Psychology's Assault On The Bible

by

David L. Brown, Ph.D.

DEDICATION

This Book is dedicated to God, my Savior Jesus Christ and the Holy Spirit. Allow a brief explanation. I attended Bible College when the rage was to be a "Christian" psychologist. I originally thought that was the path I wanted to pursue! I wasted hours taking psychology classes, reading psychology books written from a secular and "Christian" perspective and learning to administer psychological tests. However, as I studied the Word of God, the Holy Spirit of God drove home the truth of **2 Peter 1:2-3**. The Lord changed the direction of my life and called me to Preach The Word! As verse three says –

> 3 *"According as his divine power hath given unto us all things that pertain unto life and godliness, through the knowledge of him that hath called us to glory and virtue."*

My Bible opened to 2 Peter 1:2-3

2 "Grace and peace be multiplied unto you through the knowledge of God, and of Jesus our Lord, 3 According as his divine power hath given unto us all things that pertain unto life and godliness, through the knowledge of him that hath called us to glory and virtue." **2 Peter 1:2-3**

TABLE OF CONTENTS

CHAPTER ONE
INTRODUCTION

The cure for the sinful soul and the problems of life was the vital ministry of the church, using the Word of God, for more than 1900 years.

The early Church faced and ministered to mental-emotional behavioral problems that were as complex as the ones that exist today. If anything, the conditions were more difficult than those we face today. The early church suffered persecution, poverty, and various afflictions which are foreign to most twentieth-century Christians (especially in the West). The catacombs of Rome are a testimony to the extent of the problems faced by the early Church.[1]

But, as in every generation, there are those who do not want to submit to the Word of God. Freud and Jung were two such individuals from their generation. They boldly rejected the authority of the Word of God, but they did not stop there. They developed a theory that they claimed offered an alternative solution for the sin problem and the problems of life. It was called psychology. Freud and Jung believed that they had found a means through which the soul of man could be perfected without having to repent of sin and submit to God. Man didn't need Jesus as his Savior; he could be his own Savior.

From this root, psychology has grown by leaps and bounds with more than *250* separate systems of psychotherapy. But what is even more mind-boggling is that the Christian church has been duped into buying into this human wisdom. There are many Christians that have been convinced that the difficult problems of life need more than Word of God and the indwelling presence of the Holy Spirit. However, the Bible assures us,

> *"According as his divine power hath given unto us all things that pertain unto life and godliness, through the knowledge of him that hath called us to glory and virtue:"* **2 Peter 1:3**

and

> *"Thou wilt keep him in perfect peace, whose mind is stayed on thee.. because he trusteth in thee."* **Isaiah 26:3**.

Non-believers can only attain spiritual life and health by surrender to Jesus Christ as Savior and Lord. That is the direction the church should be pointing them. Psychological techniques, even in the name of Jesus, cannot produce spiritual life. It's time we get back to the Bible![2]

The church must minister under unction of the Holy Spirit—not according to man's wisdom. The problem is that many churches and Christians have been *spoiled* by the humanly devised philosophy of psychology.

> *Beware lest any man spoil you through philosophy and vain deceit, after the tradition of men, after the rudiments of the world, and not after Christ.* **Colossians 2:8**

Examining Some Of The Words of Colossians 2:8

The key word in this verse is **spoil**. When we hear the word, we think it means *"to become unfit for use or consumption, as from decay."* But that is not the meaning of the word in the New Testament context. The word *spoil* is translated from the Greek word sulagogeo, (soo-lag-ogue-eh'-o—Strongs #4812) which means *"to carry off as a captive and a slave."* Zodhiates says in *The Complete Word Study Dictionary of the New Testament* that the word means *"to carry away. To lead off as prey...rob, or kidnap. Figuratively, (used) of the destructive effects of false teachers who rob believers of the complete riches available in Christ and revealed in the gospel.*

- ***Philosophy*** (5385)-- The Greek word philosophia (fil-os-of-ee'-ah) actually means a friend to wisdom or love of wisdom. The word came to mean the doctrines, beliefs, ideologies of the unsaved and Gentile philosophers.

- *Vain* (2756) means hollow, empty, meaningless.
- *Deceit* (539) means anything that is deceptive.
- *Tradition* (3862)— An ideology, belief, doctrine or instruction communicated from one to another. In this verse the ideologies are those developed by men.
- *Rudiments* (4747)—Rudiments means principles or basics. In this context these principles are derived from the minds of lost men.

Now, when I put it all together I believe Paul was sounding this warning...

Watch out! You will encounter numerous people promoting deceptive, empty man-made ideas that sound good but are based on the world's wisdom and not God's wisdom. If you are not discerning, you will be brainwashed and be led away from the sufficiency that is in Christ.

Note the next two verses. **Colossians 2:9-10**

9 For in him dwelleth all the fullness of the Godhead bodily 10 And ye are complete in him, which is the head of all principality and power:

Though there are many philosophies that have wormed their way into Bible believing Churches, organizations and the thinking of Christians, none has undermined the Word of God and the sufficiency of Christ like psychology, with the exception of the theory of Evolution.

CHAPTER TWO
THREE FORCES

**(That Led To Psychology Replacing the Scripture
In Offering Answers To The Problems Of Life)**

What were the forces or roots that led to psychology replacing the Scripture in offering answers to the problems of life? There are three forces or roots that we need to consider.

1. The Theology of Aquinas

2. The Philosophy of Empiricism

3. The Theory of Evolution

THE FIRST FORCE THAT PREPARED THE WAY FOR PSYCHOLOGY

The Theology of Aquinas

Thomas Aquinas (1225-1274) the Italian Dominican friar and Roman Catholic priest is considered by many people to be the outstanding philoso-pher-theologian of his day. I would not agree. His theology was corrupt. The Bible says, *"the little foxes, that spoil the* vines..." (**Song of Songs 2:15**). Or to put it another way, *"A little leaven leaveneth the whole lump."* (**Galatians 5:9**). <u>His theology was tainted by the wisdom of the world</u> which is foolishness with God (**1 Corinthians 3:19**). There are at least:

Three Ways in Which Aquinas' Theology Was Corrupted.

First

He did **not** believe in the **full depravity of man**. When I refer to the "full depravity of man" I mean that **man is wholly a sinner**. Sin has touched every aspect of man—his body, mind-intellect, emotions, and will, or volition (**Romans 3:10-20**).

When Aquinas studied the fall of Adam and Eve, he concluded that though man's will was damaged by sin, *man's intellect was undamaged by sin*. Therefore, Aquinas taught *"that man, out of his own resources, could search for, find, and classify truth."*[3]

Simply stated, Aquinas believed that man's wisdom could be trusted. I can almost hear the hiss of the serpent. If Aquinas would have looked ahead a few chapters further than the account of the fall of our first parents, he would have been able to see that **sin did damage man's intellect**! **Genesis 6:5-6:**

> *And God saw that the wickedness of man was great in the earth, and that **every imagination of the thoughts of his heart was only evil continually*** *6 And it repented the LORD that he had made man on the earth, and it grieved him at his heart.* **Genesis 6:5-6**

The plain fact is, man's wisdom apart from God is, at best, vain. **1 Corinthians 3:18-20**

> *Let no man deceive himself. If any man among yo seemeth to be wise in this world, let him become a fool, that he may be wise. 19 For the wisdom of this world is foolishness with God. For it is written, He taketh the wise in their own craftiness. 20 And again, The Lord knoweth the thoughts of the wise, that they are vain.*

(See also *James 3:15-17*).

The lie that man is not totally depraved but can trust his intellect is one part of the leaven that led to the belief that mankind can find truth within himself.

Second

The **second** way the theology of Aquinas was corrupted was by his study of the **Greek philosopher, Aristotle.** Aristotle lived between 384-322 B.C. He was a pupil of Plato, the tutor of

Alexander the Great, and the author of works on logic, metaphysics, ethics, natural sciences, politics, and poetics. Aristotle profoundly influenced Western thought. In Aristotle's philosophical system **truth is discovered by empirical observation and logic**, based on the syllogism (sound reasoning). This method of inquiry leaves God out. Aquinas became an <u>Aristotelian Thinker when he should have become a BIBLICAL THINKER</u>. **2 Corinthians 10:4-5:**

> *"For the weapons of our warfare are not carnal but mighty through God to the pulling down of strong holds;) 5 Casting down imaginations, and every high thing that exalteth itself against the knowledge of God, and bringing into captivity every thought to the obedience of Christ."*

Third

Thirdly, Aquinas mixed the humanistic philosophy of Aristotle with the truth of the Bible. "Aquinas did not differentiate between what the Bible taught about life, truth, and the answers to man's problems <u>and</u> what Aristotle taught"[4] though there is a vast difference! One is based on man's wisdom and one is based on God's wisdom. As a result, Aquinas **syncretized** the Bible and the godless philosophy of Aristotle.

Syncretism Defined *n.* **1.** Reconciliation or fusion of differing systems of belief, as in philosophy or religion, especially when success is partial or the result is heterogeneous. Therefore, you end up with a new belief that is neither one nor the other previous beliefs.

THE SECOND FORCE THAT PREPARED THE WAY FOR PSYCHOLOGY

The Philosophy of Empiricism

If you go back to the beginning of empiricism, back to Greco-Roman times, those who followed this philosophy were skeptical of all theoretical explanations unless these theories could be verified by the human senses. By the 1800s this popularly held philosophy asserted that **man can only know truth by the five senses: sight, hearing, touch, taste and smell**. Everything else was a product of the imagination. The most important statement of this theory was made by **John Locke** (1632-1704). He claimed that *all knowledge comes from sense*

experience. You might wonder, what's wrong with that? **Empiricism does away with the spiritual nature of man, as well as the existence of God**. Man becomes only <u>a material being</u>. Empiricism leads to complete skepticism when it comes to God and the spiritual nature of man.

THE FINAL FORCE THAT PREPARED THE WAY FOR PSYCHOLOGY

The Theory of Evolution

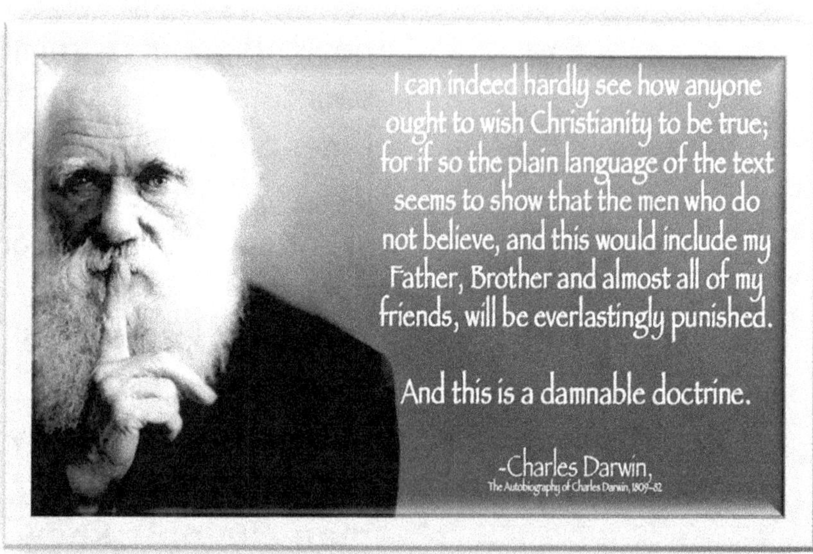

<u>Charles Darwin </u>rejected biblical Christianity. On November 24, 1859 he published - *On the Origin of Species by Means of Natural Selection, or the Preservation of Favoured Races in the Struggle for*

Life. He theorized that <u>man evolved from lower animals</u>. The degeneration was now complete. 1) Aquinas undermined the Bible's teaching on sin. 2) Empiricism took away with man's soul and 3) Evolution made man just another animal. God was now, for all practical purposes, out of the picture. Man was ready for psychology.

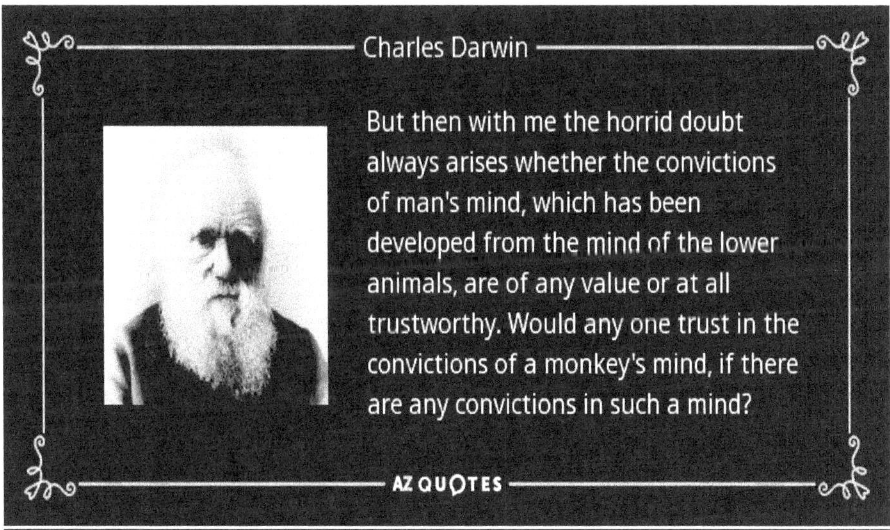

CHAPTER THREE

THE FOUR MAIN STREAMS OF PSYCHOLOGY

1. Psychoanalytic -- Sigmund Freud & Carl Jung

2. Behavioristic -- B. F. Skinner

3. Humanistic -- Carl Rogers

4. Existential or Transpersonal -- Abraham Maslow

Let's look at each of these psychological models.

THE FIRST MAJOR PSYCHOLOGICAL THEORY
PSYCHOANALYTIC PSYCHOLOGY

Very Few people are aware of the fact that Sigmund Freud (1856-1939) was involved in the occult. He was a member of the *Society of Psychical Research London* and the *American Society for Psychical Research in New York City*.

Freud had experiences with <u>clairaudience</u> (the supposed power to hear things outside the range of normal perception), <u>telepathy</u> (communication through means other than the senses, as by the exercise of an occult power), <u>dreams of premonition</u>, as well as <u>hearing voices</u> (Harpers's Encyclopedia of Mystical & Paranormal Experiences by Rosemary Guiley). It comes as no surprise that Freud also *rejected the truth that man was a sinner* and that sin was at the root of man's problems. As a result of that, he developed his own theory called the **<u>psychoanalytic theory</u>**. He said that man's problems stem from repressed desires. He supposed that the unconscious was a vast reservoir of forgotten experiences and repressed desires primarily sexual in nature. Because of this, he believed that <u>people were not really responsible for their actions</u>. Those who follow Freud say that the only way to resolve our problems is to go on an archaeological dig into your subconscious mind and see what you can dredge up from the reservoir of your unconsciousness. How did Freud attempt to get the repressed information to the surface?

First, by hypnotism. *"As a young physician, Freud* had *observed that hysterical patients seemed to lose their symptoms after being under hypnosis and recalling material which, apparently had been* *completely forgotten. From this, he developed the concept of an unconscious which dominates the activities of a person, and is motivated by forgotten experiences, forgotten by means of repression, and kept submerged by means of resistance"*[5]

Secondly, Freud developed a technique called psychoanalysis. **Psychoanalysis** is based on the assumption that various disorders of the mind are the result of the rejection by the conscious mind of factors that persist in the unconscious (repressed memories) and therefore cause internal conflict. By using <u>dream analysis</u> and <u>free association</u> he claimed these conflicts could be resolved. The natural question is, what is <u>dream analysis</u>? Freud's theory was that *"dreams are the expression of unconscious thoughts which are repressed when a person is fully awake."*[6] Therefore he concluded that he could analyze these dreams and get information about the unconscious motivations of the individual.

What about <u>free association</u>? Free association is *"the technique of having the patient talk as freely as possible bringing in whatever ideas, memories, etc. are associated in his mind."*[7] The counselor then analyzes what has been said and uses the information to "uncover" and "clarify" repressed memories.

I see major problems, don't you? The counselor is the final authority and interpretations would be evaluated on the basis of the counselor's value system.

Someone is going to say, "No one uses Freudian psychology today." Oh yes they do! A middle age single woman I have known for a number of years was having trouble with tension and sleeping. She sought out professional help. After an hour session of "free association" the conclusion of this "professional" was that she had a buildup of sexual tension. She was shocked when he suggested, and I am quoting exactly, *"the best thing that you could do would be to go out and get laid."* She was incensed that she had to pay for this psychological advice! <u>Freudian psychology is still around</u>!

The Psychiatric Folk Song by <u>Anna Russell</u> characterizes the influence of Freudian psychology in America:

- I went to my psychiatrist to be psychoanalyzed
- To find out why I killed the cat and blackened my wife's eyes.
- He put me on a downy couch to see what he could find,
- And this is what he dredged up from my subconscious mind:
- When I was one, my mommy hid my dolly in the trunk,

- And so it follows naturally that I am always drunk.
- When I was two I saw my father kiss the maid one day,
- And that is why I suffer now from kleptomania.
- When I was three, I suffered from ambivalence toward my brothers, So it follows naturally, I poison all my lovers.
- I'm so glad that I have learned the lesson it has taught,
- That everything I do that's wrong is someone else's fault!

Despite the teaching of Freud the Bible is clear. **We are responsible for our own actions** and we will all give account of ourselves to God (**Romans 14:12**). There will be no passing the buck when sinners stand before God.

Before I move on, I want to introduce you to **Carl Jung** (1875-1961). Jung broke with Freud over sexual repression being the primary root of our problems but still believed the unconscious was the root of our problems. **Jung was a Christ rejecter**. At an early age *"he renounced the austere and formal Protestant Christianity in*

which he was raised."[8] He instead exposed himself to seances and persistent poltergeist activity. *"He had his first psychic vision at the age of three."*[9] And He also affirmed *"the reality of spirits and spiritualism, on the evidence of telekinesis, messages of dying people, hypnotism, clairvoyance and prophetic dreams."*[10]

Now, fasten your seat belt, because Carl Jung gave a startling revelation near the end of his life. He candidly admitted that, *"far from being the science he had represented them to be, everything ('all my works, all my creative activity') derived from horrendous experiences with haunting spirit entities that nearly drove him insane. It was during this time that 'Philemon' became his 'spirit guide.'"*[11]

Jung was involved in Gnosticism, Alchemy, Astrology, I Ching, Mystical Systems, Spiritualism & Folklore. His grandfather was a Rosicrucian.

Summary

The Psychoanalytic Theory of Psychology teaches that:

1) Man is a biological machine or biologic-psychic determinism. Man is merely a product of genetics and his environment. He is driven by forces in his subconscious mind that he can neither

understand nor control, such as sexual repression and the repression and hindering of free expression. Only by psychoanalysis can these things be uncovered and dealt with so the individual can have freedom and peace.

2) As just mentioned, the key to freedom and peace is uncovering repressed memories. This is done by hypnotism and psychoanalysis. Psychoanalysis is a combination of dream analysis and free association techniques.

3) The psychoanalytic view of right and wrong is, right and wrong are only what you determine them to be.

It should be obvious that this psychological model is diametrically opposed to Biblical teaching on the nature of man and his problems and MUST be rejected. The Bible says:

> *"Prove all things; hold fast that which is good."* **1 Thessalonians 5:21**

and

> *"Abhor that which is evil; cleave to that which is good."* **Romans 12:9**

THE SECOND MAJOR PSYCHOLOGICAL THEORY
BEHAVIORISTIC PSYCHOLOGY

Let's move on to the **second major psychological theory**. This theory is called the Behavioristic theory. It was developed by B. F. Skinner (1904-1990). Skinner looked at man from an evolutionary point of view. Man was just an animal. The way to solve man's problems was by behavioral modification, a system of rewards and punishment. This would enable man to better fit into the social order designed by the intellectually elite.

Summary

Here is a short summary of the Behavioristic Psychology theory. Man is just a soulless animal who has no free will and no guarantee of meaning or happiness in life. As an animal, behavioral modification is what is needed to solve the problems of life. When his behavior is modified, man will be enabled to better fit into the orderly society of the intellectually elite.

The problems of life are solved by behavior modification so the person can fall into lock-step with the "politically correct" norm. Their view of *right and wrong is -- <u>Right and wrong are determined by the intellectually elite</u>.*

In fact, we are not animals and we are not the product of evolution! The Bible says in **Genesis 1:27:**

"...God created man in his own image, in the image of God created he him; male and female created he them."

THE THIRD MAJOR PSYCHOLOGICAL THEORY
HUMANISTIC PSYCHOLOGY

The **third theory** was developed by <u>Carl Rogers (1902-1987).</u> His theory is called the <u>Humanistic Psychology</u>. In this view, <u>problems stem from our conscience and guilt</u>. These two things (guilt & conscience) need to be done away with because they are holding back our freedom, creativity and joy. What we need to do is love ourselves and accept ourselves because <u>self-love & self-acceptance is the key to solving our problems</u>.

Summary

Here is a short summary of the Humanistic Theory of Psychology. Man is good and has unlimited potential! Yet, people are not responsible for what they are, but they have a free will and can choose to change. The problems that man have stem from conscience and guilt. These two must be done away with because they keep us back from freedom, creativity and joy. What we need is non-judgmental self-acceptance. Further we must realize that the answer to all our problems lies within ourselves. The key to problem solving in this model is self-acceptance. Self is elevated to godhood, because you have all the answers to your problems within yourself. Further, there is no right and wrong in this psychological model. What is right for you is right and what is wrong for you is wrong. But why did Rogers adopt such an anti-biblical view? While he was in seminary studying for the ministry he rebelled against God, renounced the Bible and discarded his conservative Protestant upbringing. He rejected the biblical view of man and offered his second-rate substitute. **1 Samuel 15:23** says, *For rebellion is as the sin of witchcraft..."* so it is little wonder that later in his life, when he came face to face with eternity that he took to attending seances and looked to the Ouija board for answers about the hereafter.

Our greatest need is not to love ourselves and accept ourselves, our greatest need it to be right with God, get saved and live for him. It is far more important that God accepts us than to spend our time learning how better to accept ourselves. **Note Matthew 16:24:**

> *Then said Jesus unto his disciples, If any man will come after me, let him deny himself, and take up his cross, and follow me.*

THE FOURTH MAJOR PSYCHOLOGICAL THEORY
SELF-ACTUALIZATION

Finally, we come to the last major psychological theory developed by Abraham Maslow (1908-1970). This view is called Existential or Transpersonal Psychology.

In Maslow's view there were **no absolutes**. You determine your own reality. The answer to your problems is **Self-Actualization**, discovering that **you are "god**." You just need to accept that fact and live accordingly. *American Health* magazine sums this view up quite well when it said, *"There's a new breed of shrinks in the land. But instead of couches* and *Rorschach tests,* *their accouterments are tarot cards and astrological charts... [These are] the shrinks of the yuppie generation... belief in the occult is stronger than ever.* "[12]

Summary

Here is a short summary of the Existential Theory of Psychology -- Man is a spiritual being, capable of making his own reality. The answer to our problems is self-actualization, that is, we need to discover the "god" within ourselves. The cure for our problems comes from mystical practices, occult meditation, and many other practices associated with Eastern Religions. Once you realize that you are god and accept that fact, you will have fulfillment. In this view, your determine right and wrong. There are no absolutes.

Why do people go to psychologists and psychiatrists, and does it help?

"The truth is, most people go to psychologists and psychiatrists looking for help with the problems of life. "Research psychiatrist E. Fuller Torrey found that about 5% of those who come to a psychiatrist are people with organic brain disease while about 75% are people with problems of living. 20% will require closer examination to make a final judgment to determine which category they fit into. Torrey continues that at least 75% of those who come to a psychiatrist do not need treatment but actually need to be educated in how to live." [13]

Frankly, I would estimate that by the time the remaining 20% of the cases are examined that at least 15% would fit in to the *"need to be educated in how to live"* category, bringing the total to 90%. This study shows that most people are looking in the wrong place for help. The Bible has the answers for life's problems. Therefore, they need to look to the Bible and a biblical counselor for help.

Now, is psychology helping the people who seek out its advice? Research shows that psychology is not doing such a good job at resolving the problems of life. *The Joint Commission on Mental Illness and Health* did a survey and this is what they found—*"of those persons who actively sought help for personal problems, the vast majority contacted persons other than mental health professionals, and generally they were more satisfied with the help they received than were those who chose psychiatrists and psychologists."*[14]

Oil and water don't mix. Holy and unholy don't mix. Psychology and the Bible don't mix. Psychology is being offered and accepted as the answer to the problems of life in the censers of many Bible believing churches across our land and the Lord is grieved. We must get back to the Bible for our answers. Likely, there will be some who don't want to hear what I have just shared with you. Consider **Galatians 4:16:**

> *Am I therefore become your enemy, because I tell you the truth?*

Friends, psychology is a humanly devised fable and should be rejected! **2 Timothy 4:3-4** says:

> *3 For the time will come when they will not endure sound doctrine; but after their own lusts shall they heap to themselves teachers, having itching ears; 4 And they shall turn away their ears from the truth, and shall be turned unto fables.*

Today, the Bible is being replaced by psychology as the standard for dealing with the problems of life. Many pastors are giving their people a steady diet of psycho-babel from the pulpit and in their counseling. In fact, the most listened to theologian in America today is not a theologian at all. Dr. James Dobson is a psychologist. While I appreciate Dr. Dobson's intervention on behalf of the family, there is a problem. He's got a whole generation believing that the root of their problems in life is that they don't love and accept themselves enough. That's not what the Bible says (**Eph. 5:29;**

Phil. 2:3; James 2:8). Our problem is that we love ourselves too much. Man's greatest need is to be right with God, not to love ourselves and accept ourselves more. Offering psychological solutions for the problems of life is strange fire because that is not where we have been commanded to go!

Where have we been commanded to go? To the Bible! Since God created us, He knows what makes us tick. God has provided us with reliable information on *"how to live?"* **2Peter 1:2-4** says:

> *2 Grace and peace be multiplied unto you through the knowledge of God, and of Jesus our Lord, 3 According as his divine power hath given unto us all things that pertain unto life and godliness, through the knowledge of him that hath called us to glory and virtue: 4 whereby are given unto us exceeding great and precious promises: that by these ye might be partakers of the divine nature, having escaped the corruption that is in the world through lust.*

This passage simply says that God has provided all that we need to live a victorious, God-honoring life. As a person looks to God and the guidance given in His Word, then implements the principles that he finds there, he will change in the areas of thoughts, emotions and actions—he will learn how to live. Why can I say that with authority? **2 Timothy 3:16-17** says:

> *16 All scripture is given by inspiration of God* (God breathed), *and is profitable* (a useful guide) *for doctrine* (what's right) *, for reproof (what's not right), for correction* (how to get right), *for instruction* (how to stay right) *in righteousness: 17 That the man of God may be perfect* (whole), *throughly furnished* (competent) *unto all good works.*

Simply stated, the Bible tells us what's right, what's not right, how to get right and how to stay right. That is what people need today!

All four key streams of psychological theories are based on man's wisdom, the wisdom from beneath which is in direct opposition to God's wisdom. **James 3:15-17** describes the two sources of wisdom:

> *15 This wisdom descendeth not from above, but is earthly, sensual, devilish. 16 For where envying and strife' is, there is confusion and every evil work 17 But the wisdom that is from above is first pure, then peaceable, gentle, and easy to be entreated, full of mercy and good fruits, without partiality, and without hypocrisy.*

The Bible clearly points out what God thinks of this world's wisdom:

> *"For the wisdom of this world is foolishness with God.."* **1 Corinthians 3:19**

END NOTES

1. Martin & Deidre Bobgin; *Psychology -- Science or Religion;* *p.3*

2. Albert James Dager; *Inner Healing -- A Biblical Analysis;* *p.13*

3. Nelson E. Hinman; *An Answer To Humanistic Psychology;* Harvest House Publishers

4. Ibid.

5. Franklin Dunham - Editor; *The New Universal One-Volume Encyclopedia;* p.637

6. Ibid.

7. *Webster's New World Dictionary of the American* Language - 1968, p. 557

8. Hunt & McMahon; *America: The Sorcerer's New Apprentice;* p.11

9. Ibid.

10. C. G. Jung; *Psychology and The Occult;* Princeton University Press - 1977; p. vii

11. Hunt & McMahon; *America: The Sorcerer's New Apprentice;* p.11

12. Lise Spiegel; *American Health Magazine - New Age Shrinks;* p. 18

13. Joint Commission On Mental Health - *Action for Mental Health;* p. 103

14. Bergin & Lambert; *Handbook of Psychotherapy and Behavior Change -- The Evaluation of Therapeutic Outcomes;* p. 149

CHAPTER 4

GENERAL SCRIPTURES FOR BIBLICAL COUNSELING

(Adapted from materials published by the Institute for Biblical Counseling & Discipleship)

I. General principles

A. The Bible is infallible and sufficient for counseling. 2 Tim 3:16-17

B. Apply the gospel specifically to every problem. Phil 4:12

C. You and your counselee are totally dependent upon God for success. John 15:5

II. Addressing various counseling problems

A. Conflict resolution

1. Pursue peace. Matt 5:9 2.

2. Listen carefully and listen to both sides. Prov 18:13,17

3. First address your own sin. Matt 7:3-5

4. Confront your erring brother in love. Gal 6:1-2

5. Be prepared to follow the steps of church discipline. Matt 18:15-20

6. Christians should not sue other Christians in secular courts. 1 Cor 6:1f

7. Even if you do all you can to seek resolution, you may not succeed. Rom 12:18

B. Anger

1. Anger is murder. Matt 5:21-22

2. The cause of conflict is sinful desire. Jas 4:1-6

3. An angry person is dangerous. Prov 25:28

C. Revenge

1. Don't take your own revenge. Trust God to do what is right. Rom 12:19-21

2. Show love to your enemy. Matt 5:43-48

D. Helping people who have been hurt by others (abused)

1. Bitterness is destructive. Heb 12:15

2. Joseph trusted God and thereby forgave his abusers. Gen 50:19-20

E. Communication

1. The tongue is a fire. Jas 3:6f

2. Use your words to build up, not tear down. Don't always say whatever is on your mind. Eph 4:29

3. Be slow to speak and quick to listen. Jas 1:19-20

4. Focus on understanding the other person rather than upon being understood. Phil 2:3-4

5. A soft answer turns away wrath. Prov 15:1

F. Resisting temptation

1. God's promise: you won't be tempted beyond what you are able. 1 Cor 10:13

2. Joseph's example. Gen 39:7-10

G. Lust

1. Lust in the heart is adultery. Matt 5:27-30

2. Flee lust. 2 Tim 2:22

3. You are responsible for what you think about. Phil 4:8-9 (also applies to fear, worry, depression, etc.)

H. Fear

1. The fear of man brings a snare. Prov 29:25

2. Trusting in people is idolatry and will ruin you. Jer 17:5-8

I. Worry

1. Trust God to meet your needs. Matt 6:25-34

2. Pray with thanksgiving. Phil 4:6-7

J. Depression

1. Are you depressed because of your sin? Ps 32

2. The key to overcoming depression is not a change in your circumstances, but an increase in your faith. Phil 4:11-13

K. Addictions

1. Addiction is seeking from some idol what God alone gives. Isa 55:1-2

2. The root problem is that some love pleasure more than they love God. 2 Tim 3:4

3. Substance abuse is sinful and destructive. Prov 23:29-35

4. "Co-dependents" make the addict their idol. Jer 17:5-8

L. Facing trials and calamity

1. God sovereignly works all things together for good. Rom 8:28

2. God uses trials in your sanctification. Jas 1:2f

3. Nothing can separate you from God's love in Christ. Rom 8:31-39

M. Seeking forgiveness

1. From God. 1 John 1:8-10

2. From those you have wronged. Matt 5:23-24

N. Granting forgiveness

1. Forgive as you have been forgiven. Eph 4:32

2. The account of the unmerciful servant. Matt 18:21-35

O. Repentance

1. How can you tell if repentance is genuine? 2 Cor 7:9-11

2. An example of true repentance. Ps 51

P. Presenting the Gospel

1. We are saved not by keeping the law, but by Christ's atoning death. Rom 3:20-26

2. Confess your sins. 1 John 1:8-2:2

3. The substitution of the Lamb of God for sinners. Isa 53:4-6

4. The thief on the cross as an example of salvation by grace. Luke 23:39-43 5. We are saved by grace alone through faith alone. Eph 2:8-9

Q. Assurance of salvation

1. If you truly believe in the Lord Jesus, you have been born of God. 1 John 5:1

2. If you are one of Christ's sheep, He keeps you safe. John 10:28-29

3. If you have no regard for God's commandments you are still lost. 1 John 2:3-4

4. If you have no love for the brethren, you have not been born of God. 1 John 4:8-9

R. Sanctification

1. The converted sinner is no longer to be labeled by his old deeds. 1 Cor 6:9- 11

2. Consider your old nature dead and your new nature alive in Christ. Rom 6:11

3. The believer is a new person with a new nature. 2 Cor 5:17

4. God will work to sanctify you. Phil 1:6

5. You are responsible to put forth effort in your sanctification. Phil 2:12-13

6. Learn and apply the put off and put on dynamic. Eph 4:22-24

7. Christ saved us that we might do good works. Titus 2:14

S. Church involvement

1. Regular attendance is mandatory. Heb 10:25

2. God wants you to commit (join), making yourself accountable to particular church leaders. Heb 13:17

3. Each of us is to serve. 1 Pet 4:10-11

4. Each of us is to give as God has prospered us. 1 Cor 16:2

T. Work and employment

1. God's design is that you work six days a week. Exod 20:9

2. Don't be a sluggard. Prov 6:6-11

3. If someone refuses to work, he should not eat. 2 Thess 3:10

4. Serve God through your vocation. Eph 6:5-9

U. Finances

1. Planning (budgeting) is wise. Prov 21:5

2. Acknowledge God's sovereignty over your finances. Jas 4:13-17

3. God gives you the ability to earn. Deut 8:18

4. Avoid debt. Prov 22:7

5. Don't make an idol of money, but store up treasure in heaven. Matt 6:19-21

6. The love of money leads to every other evil behavior. 1 Tim 6:10

7. Be generous with those in need. 1 Tim 6:17-19

8. Giving to the Lord's work should be the first item in your budget. Prov 3:9

9. Pay your taxes. Matt 22:17-21

V. Decision Making/Knowing God's will

1. Wholeheartedly seek wisdom from God. Jas 1:5 (also see Prov 1-9).

2. Search for God's moral will in the Bible. 2 Tim 3:16-17

3. Seek godly counsel. Prov 15:22

4. You can't know God's secret will. Deut 29:29

5. Submit your plans to God's sovereign will. Prov 16:9

6. Trust God, that His way is best. Prov 3:5-6

W. Integrity

1. Simply tell the truth. Matt 5:37

2. Lying destroys relationships. Eph 4:25

III. Family issues

A. Marriage is divinely instituted

1. God's design for marriage. Gen 2:18-23

2. God's directive for marriage. Gen 2:24

B. The role of the husband

1. Loving. Eph 5:25-30

2. Leading. Eph. 4:2, 1 Cor. 11:3

2. Understanding. 1 Pet 3:7

3. Serving. John 13:1f

C. The role of the wife

1. Submission. Eph 5:22-24

2. Dealing with an unsaved husband. 1 Pet 3:1-6 (see context 2:21-25)

D. Sex

1. All sex outside of marriage is wrong. Heb 13:4 (also see Gen. 2:24)

2. God wants us to be fruitful (have kids). Gen 1:28

3. Your sexuality belongs to your spouse. Don't deprive him/her. 1 Cor 7:3-5

4. God wants married people to enjoy sex. Prov 5:18-19 (also Song of Solomon)

E. Child training

1. The duties of children. Eph 6:1-3

2. The duties of parents. Eph 6:4

3. The necessity of discipline. Prov 19:18

F. Divorce

1. God hates divorce. Mal 2:16

2. What God has joined, let no man separate. Matt 19:5-6

3. Don't leave your unbelieving spouse or drive him/her away. 1 Cor 7:12

4. If you divorce there is no permission to remarry – Rom. 7:2-3

6. Remarriage is allowable if the spouse is dead. 1 Cor.   7:39

WHERE WILL YOU SPEND ETERNITY?

"Well," you ask, "how would I know?" Thank God, according to the Bible, not only can you *know*, but you can *choose* where you will spend eternity.

Now we all believe – or at least most claim to believe – in the Bible as God's Word. We believe in eternity and know that life is short. The Bible itself asks, "What is your life? It is even a vapor, that appeareth for a little time, and then vanisheth away" (James 4:14).

Many claim to believe in heaven and in hell, yet, unfortunately, show little concern over their eternal destiny. We are far more concerned about this life than the next, yet we know that eternity is endless. The Word of God describes it as being "forever and ever" (Revelation 22:5).

Just think . . . an eternity to be spent forever, either in the perfect paradise called heaven or in the terrible torments of hell.

Surely we'll agree that it is just good sense to prepare for eternity now, before it is forever too late. God says, "It is appointed unto men once to die, but after this the judgment" (Hebrews 9:27).

"Well," you say, "I believe in God, go to church, and live the best I can. What else can I do?"

Now believing in God, attending church, and doing one's best are all admirable; yet, according to the Word of God, the Holy Bible, these *cannot* get us to heaven. Neither, according to God, can our church membership, baptism, confirmation, nor our good deeds attain for us eternal life.

But God has provided an answer to the matter of life and death, heaven and hell. It is an answer so simple it is frequently overlooked.

A religious leader named Nicodemus came to Jesus one night for help. Jesus told him, "You must be born again," and expanded this to include all of us by stating quite emphatically, "Except a man be born again, he cannot see the kingdom of God" (John 3:3). Pretty dogmatic perhaps, but these are the words of Christ Himself.

Some today, like Nicodemus, will ask, "How can a man be born when he is old? Can he enter the second time into his mother's womb, and be born?" (John 3:4). But Jesus answers, "That which is born of the flesh is flesh; and that which is born of Spirit is spirit" (John 3:6), stating again that one must experience a spiritual rebirth in order to enter heaven – "You *must* be born again" (John 3:7).

Now, have *you* been born again? Have you experienced this spiritual rebirth? This is the one thing, according to the Bible, that will determine your eternal destiny.

So, for those who really want to know how to be born again, here is the answer from God's Word.

We must **recognize that we are sinners,** that we've all violated God's law. The Bible says, "All have sinned, and come short of the glory of God . . . There is not a just man upon earth, that doeth good, and sinneth not . . . If we say that we have no sin, we deceive ourselves, and the truth is not in us" (Romans 3:23, 10; Ecclesiastes 7:20; I John 1:8, 10).

We must **repent of our sins.** The Bible says that God "commandeth all men everywhere to repent" (Acts 17:30). Jesus said, "Except you repent, you shall all likewise perish" (Luke 13:3). And it is not so difficult to repent as we pause to think of what our sins have cost God. It was for our sins that God, the Creator and King of this universe, left His home in heaven and came to earth in the Person of the Lord Jesus to suffer and bleed and die – that we might be forgiven. "Hereby perceive we the love of God, because He laid down His life for us" (I John 3:16).

Then Jesus rose from the dead, proving His victory over sin and death.

We must **receive Christ into our hearts and lives as our Savior.** We read in the first chapter of John, speaking of the Lord Jesus, "He was in the world, and the world was made by Him, and the world knew Him not. He came unto His own, and His own received Him not. But as many as *received* Him, to them gave He power to become the sons of God, even to them that believe on His name" (John 1:10-12). The moment we open our hearts to the Lord Jesus and place our complete trust in Him – and Him alone – as our Savior, God promises to forgive our sins, save our soul, and reserve for us a home in heaven. Then, on the authority of the Word of God, **we can *know* where we'll spend eternity.** God says, "These things have I written unto you that believe on the name of the Son of God; that you may *know* that you *have* eternal life" (I John 5:13). And Jesus promises, "He that heareth My word, and believeth on Him that sent Me, hath everlasting life, and shall not come into condemnation; but is passed from death unto life" (John 5:24).

Now, are you willing to settle the matter of your eternal destiny? Will you do it? You can, right this moment. I sincerely hope that you will. (*Used by permission of The American Tract Society, Garland, Texas)*

53

ABOUT THE AUTHOR

David L. Brown was born in Michigan. He came to know Christ as his Savior as the result of a Sunday school teacher throwing away the liberal curriculum, teaching through the book of Romans, and sharing the Gospel. He has been married to Linda, a young lady from his home church, for 55 years. Thy have 3 children, 13 grandchildren and 7 great grandchildren.

David attended a Michigan University and then transferred to a Christian University and Seminary where he completed a Bachelor's Degree in Social Science and Theology. He holds a Master's Degree in Theology, and Ph.D. in History, specializing in the history of the English Bible.

For 45 years he Pastored of the First Baptist Church of Oak Creek, Wisconsin (an independent, fundamental, Baptist Church using the King James Bible and conservative music). Previously he pastored an independent Baptist Church in Michigan for five years, was an assistant pastor for 4 years, and served with his wife as short term missionaries in Haiti.

Currently, Dr. Brown travels nationally and internationally, teaching and preaching in Bible Colleges and Seminaries, Churches, and conferences. Topics include the history of our English Bible, defending the King James Bible, A Biblical view of social issues (Pro-Life, Socialism, Humanism, Critical Race Theory, Psychology, etc.), God's Blueprint for Dating, Marriage and Families, Unmasking the Dangers of Calvinism, Examining the End Times and more.

Dr. Brown is the president of the ***King James Bible Research Council,*** (**www.kjbrc.org**), an organization dedicated to promoting the King James Bible and its underlying texts and other traditional text translations around the world in a solid and sensible way.

He is also the president of ***Logos Communication Consortium, Inc***. (www.logosresourcepages.org), a research organization that produces a large variety of materials warning Christians of present dangers in our culture.

Dr. Brown is the Curator of the ***Biblical Heritage Archives*** and regularly takes his rare Bible, manuscript and artifact collection to fundamental Baptist Churches teaching and preaching on the history of our English Bible, showing how God has preserved His Word(s), and why we should use the King James Bible.

General Brown is also the Vice Commander of the United States Service Command of America, which is an elite corps of highly skilled professionals training Chaplains and offering churches security training. We currently have Chaplains serving law enforcement agencies, fire rescue units, hospitals Military Entrance Processing Stations, community services and more. We also provide security personnel training for churches.

He also serves as a consultant for individuals, museums, colleges, universities, and seminaries that desire to acquire or have collections of biblical manuscripts and Bibles. He is an antiquarian book dealer with contacts around the world.

He is the author of many books and articles. Many can be found here with links and sample pages:

Brown Books (theoldpathspublications.com)

He can be contacted at:

Dr. David L. Brown
P. O. Box 173
Oak Creek, WI. 53154
Phone: 414-768-9754
Email: PastorDavidLBrown@gmail.com

OTHER WORKS BY Dr. BROWN

The Indestructible Book

The Indestructible Book, written by Dr. David L. Brown, Pastor of Oak Creek First Baptist Church in Oak Creek, WI. It is a 500 page hardback book with interior color pictures and with a dust-jacket *"The book is a very valuable tool for anyone interested in the modern debates over preservation, the Traditional Text, and the King James Bible. The greatest thing about this book is that it demonstrates clearly that we have an Indestructible Bible. It takes a lot of diligent study to "get up to speed" on the many points of controversy that are part of this discussion. This book is a great head start on understanding these issues because of Dr. Brown's knowledge and insight into them and by the way the material is presented. The Indestructible Book by Dr. David Brown reinforces, educates and strengthens our faith. It is worthy of your time and attention."* Dr. Phil Stringer

<u>God's Blueprint for Marriage and Family</u>

There is no doubt about it! God has a blueprint for building strong, successful Marriages and Families! He has clearly drawn out that blueprint in the Bible. Discover the truth in this book:

God's Blueprint for Marriage & Family:

1. God's Blueprint For Married Couples: It is God's design and will that each married couple leave their parents, cleave to each other and become intimately involved (one flesh) with each other.

2. God's Blueprint For Husbands: It is God's design and will that each husband love his own wife and lead her.

3. God's Blueprint For Wives: It is God's design and will that each wife submit to her own husband and assist, aid and complete him.

4. God's Blueprint For Communication: It is God's design and will that family members listen and talk with each other often, within the context of self-control.

5. God's Blueprint For Commitment: It is God's design and will that each family member be

committed to Christ, spouses be committed to each other, and parents be committed to their children.

6. God's Blueprint For Parents: It is God's design and will that each parent rear their children biblically, communicate with them constantly, and love them fervently.

The Dark Side of Halloween

The purpose of this book is to make you aware of the dark side of Halloween and show you how the demonic principles and practices are beguiling our children and our culture. I have researched this topic for nearly two decades and there is absolutely no doubt about Halloween's occult connection. Halloween has been the occultists' most effective tool in bewitching America! It has been and is being used by occultists of all stripes to interject their demonic doctrines into our culture.

It was 1984 when I released the first printed edition of this book under the title, Halloween: Behind The Mask. It included only 16 pages of information exposing Halloween's occult connection. As a result of that little book, I had the opportunity to present the material in churches, at rallies, in Christian schools and on Christian radio and TV programs. Many people were skeptical at first. To my surprise, some of the most antagonistic people I encountered were pastors and heads of Christian ministries and colleges. Many insisted that I was over reacting and that Halloween was just harmless fun. I must tell you, by and large, that is not the response I am getting today. Indeed "the mask" is off of the unholy day. Witches are out of the "broom closet" and peddling their demonic wares on television, in the newspapers, in the bookstores, and in the public schools. Speaking of the public schools. What is happening in your school district? I get calls from around the nation telling me that the Christian celebrations of Christmas (the birth of Christ) and Easter (the resurrection of Christ) are snubbed, maligned and even expelled from some public schools, but, not the occult holiday of Halloween! That is the public school's biggest holiday. Children are often required to write reports on witchcraft. There are public schools that have even brought in witches to tell about their "wonderful, wholesome" religion. In the public schools, witchcraft is "IN" and Christianity is "OUT." While many Christians are waking up to the dark side of Halloween, Americans in general are increasingly being exposed to occult principles and adopting occult practices. Americans are being bewitched. Now, before I jump too far ahead, let's look at The History, The Heroes and The Harm of Halloween.

Gaslighted: You Are Being Gaslighted

"Gaslighting" is used to describe abusive behavior, specifically when an abuser manipulates information in such a way as to make a victim question his or her sanity. Gaslighting intentionally makes someone doubt their memories or perception of reality. The term Gaslighting originates in the systematic psychological manipulation of a victim by her husband in Patrick Hamilton's 1938 stage play Gaslight, and the film adaptations released in 1940 and 1944. In the story, the husband attempts to convince his wife and others that she is insane by manipulating small elements of their environment and insisting that she is mistaken, remembering things incorrectly, or delusional when she points out these changes. The play's title alludes to how the abusive husband slowly dims the gas lights in their home, while pretending nothing has changed, in an effort to make his wife doubt her own perceptions. The wife repeatedly asks her husband to confirm her perceptions about the dimming lights, but in defiance of reality, he keeps insisting that the lights are the same and instead it is she who is going insane."

Critical Race Theory (In English and Spanish)

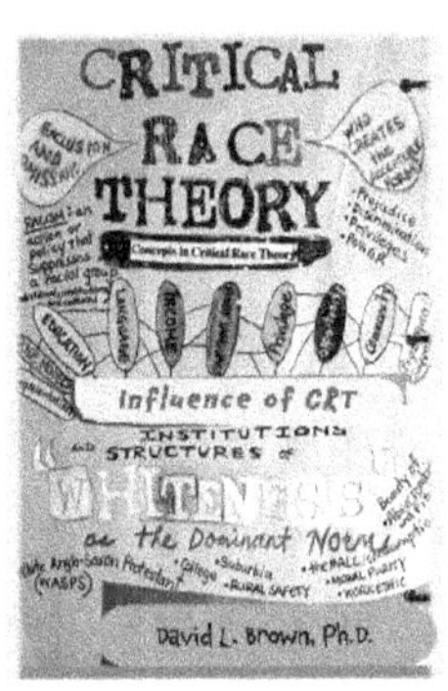

The agitation of the Black Lives Matter movement has dominated the public discourse in the United States since the death of an African American man who died during his arrest in Minneapolis. This was a tragic event. The death of Mr. Floyd was troubling indeed. However, I am also concerned over the legitimacy of the phrase "black lives matter," since all lives irrespective of race matter! Mr. Floyd's death was the spark that lit the fires of violent protests, police shootings and terrorism in many cities across the USA by groups like Black Lives Matter, Antifa and other groups and individuals. In fact, violence is being encouraged. One Black Lives Matter leader said they would burn the system down if they don't get what they want. When Philadelphia Police shot and killed Walter Wallace who refused to drop his knife and came at them October 26, 2020 people marched through the streets shouting, "Every city every town, burn the precincts to the ground." Following was looting and violence where 30 policemen were injured.

What is at the root of all of this? I believe the foundation of all of this is a philosophy called Critical Race Theory (CRT)

The Bible Source Book

The Bible Source Book can help make you a better Bible student. A Bible students tools are his Bible and his books. Here is a handy volume offering a number of methods of personal Bible study, asking with well-organized outlines of all the major Bible doctrines designed to answer your questions as you study. A concise Bible dictionary quickly defines many of the words Bible students stumble over. A practical handbook for anyone—especially new Christians. Edited by Dr. David Brown.

<u>1526 Tyndale New Testament and Biography:</u>
<u>Reprint</u>

This is a cloth bound book, 540 pages with an extensive Tyndale biography. The 1526 Tyndale New Testament is a reprint from the "Rare Book Archive" of Dr. David L. Brown's Biblical Heritage Archive Collection. William Tyndale (1492? – 1536) played a monumental role in the establishment of the Authorized Version of 1611 (i.e., King James Bible). He was the first to translate Erasmus's Greek New Testament (NT) into English and then provided the world with the first printed English NT. He stands as the greatest of all English biblical scholars. While his first edition NT was published in 1526, his second revised and corrected NT was published in 1534, two years before he was martyred. Tyndale also completed the Hebrew-to-English translation for 15 of 39 books in the Old Testament, including the Pentateuch. Tyndale published the first edition of his English New Testament in 1526. Only two full copies have survived, both pocket size. It is believed there were 3,000 printed in Worms by Peter Schoeffer. The British Library bought the copy owned by Bristol Baptist College for 1 million pounds, declaring

Tyndale's New Testament as "the most important printed book in the English language."

The second complete copy of Tyndale's 1526 New Testament was discovered in November of 1996 at the Wurttembergische Landesbibliothek (a state library) in Stuttgart, Germany. This German copy has a title page, which is missing in the British library copy. Apparently, the German library's director, Eberhard Zwink, was overseeing the library data transfer from hand-written hard copy records to computerized records. During this transition process, Zwink realized that one of the library's holdings was actually a 1526 New Testament by Tyndale.

Taken together, several research studies indicate that 83% - 90% of the King James Bible (1611, Authorized Version) can be traced to Tyndale's English translation work; specific findings suggest that 83% of the NT and 76% of the OT in the King James Bible is Tyndale's translation (The Bible in English by David Daniell, Yale University Press; The King James Version Defended by Edward Hills, Christian Research Press).

Within his small New Testament are words and phrases which have gone on to influence the world, and continue to do so today. A surprising number of Tyndale's phrases are still in common use today, including: 'under the sun', 'eat, drink and be merry', 'signs of the times', 'the salt of the earth', 'let there be light', 'my brother's keeper', 'lick the dust', 'fall flat on his face', 'the land of the living', 'pour out one's heart', 'the apple of his eye', 'fleshpots', 'go the extra mile', 'the parting of the ways', broken-hearted', 'flowing with milk and honey'.

Why Socialism is Not Biblical

"Socialism is any of various economic and political theories advocating collective or governmental ownership and administration of the means of production and distribution of goods or a system of society in which there is no private property. There are three aspects of socialism described by Dr. Brown in this treatise which are contrary to Biblical principles. Socialism is based upon a materialistic world view alone. It penalizes diligence, sanctions stealing, and promotes envy. Marxism/Socialism is a system that calls for the redistribution of wealth. Handouts destroy personal accountability and the biblical work ethic. The Bible calls for diligence and condemns laziness!"

<u>THE GENEVA BIBLE</u>

The entire Geneva Bible was released in 1560. It was innovative in both text and format, and quickly became the household Bible of English speaking people. It was the first English Bible to have modern verse divisions as well as modern chapter divisions. It was the first Bible to use italics to indicate words not in the original language and the first Bible to change the values of ancient coins into English pound sterling equivalents. It was also the first to use plain Roman type, which was more readable than the old Gothic type, and it was in a handy quarto size for easy use. With prologues before each book, extensive marginal notes, and a brief concordance, the Geneva Bible was in fact the first English "study Bible."

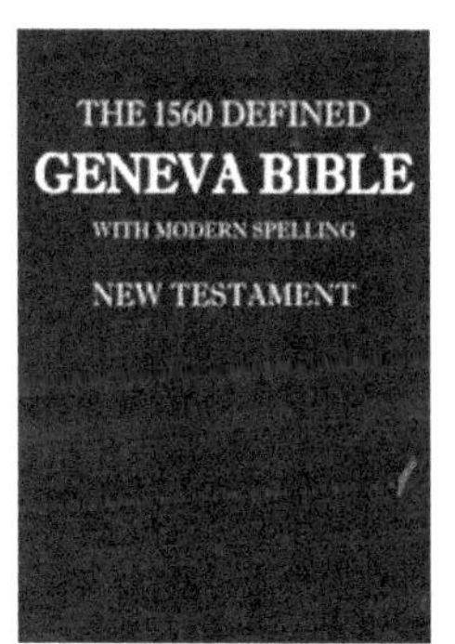

Between the Geneva Bible's first edition of 1560 and its last edition in 1644, 160 editions, totaling around a half million Bibles, were produced. And for the first time, common people could not only understand the words in the Bible, they could actually own one. Its widespread use first solidified the English language among the common people, not the 1611 King James Bible as many assume. Actually, the King James Bible required decades to surpass the popularity of the Geneva and supplant it from the hearts of the English-speaking world. In fact, the Geneva Bible was the principal English Bible initially brought to American soil, making it the Bible that shaped early American life and impacted Colonial culture more than any other.

In this edition, we have chosen not to include any commentary and simply allow the strength of the translation to come through to the reader. Yet because 450 plus years have elapsed since the original Geneva Bible, we have modernized the spelling of words. We have also bracketed and defined words and terms which are no longer commonly used or are so altered in their meaning as to be unfamiliar today.

Further, this work is not intended to replace the King James Bible, but to show how close the Geneva translation is to the King James Bible. These two Bibles are translated from the same Traditional Hebrew/Aramaic and Greek Texts. So, why was the King James Bible needed? It was because the marginal notes were "very partial," King James said. And they were. They were completely Calvinistic and many considered the notes as a part of divine revelation, which they are not. On January 17, 1604, the motion was made and carried "…that a translation be made of the whole Bible, as consonant as can be to the original Hebrew and Greek; and this to be set out and printed without any marginal notes." Only cross references, and word definitions and occasional variant reading were allowed.

After 85 years of and six English Bible translations (Tyndale, Coverdale, Matthews, Great, Bishops, Geneva) virtually all English Bible translation efforts cease for 274 years with the publication of the King James Bible. The King James Bible is the most popular book of all times. It has been in constant publication since 1611 with an estimated 6 billion copies being published. The Geneva Bible, which is virtually unknown today, played an important part in American History. It was our desire to modernize the spelling and define the archaic words so the reader easily read and see why it holds such an important place in American History.

Edited by David L. Brown and James Krueger

Dr. Brown may be contacted here:

✝

Dr. David L. Brown
P. O. Box 173
Oak Creek, WI. 53154
Phone: 414-768-9754
Email: PastorDavidLBrown@gmail.com

Dr. Brown's books may be purchased here with links to major distributors:

Brown Books
(www.theoldpathspublications.com)